BAHRAIN 2016 HUMAN RIGHTS REPORT

EXECUTIVE SUMMARY

Bahrain is a constitutional monarchy. King Hamad Bin Isa al-Khalifa, the head of state, appoints the cabinet, consisting of 26 ministers; 12 of those ministers were members of the al-Khalifa ruling family. Parliament consists of an appointed upper house, the Shura (Consultative) Council, and the elected Council of Representatives, each with 40 seats. Approximately 52 percent of eligible voters participated in parliamentary elections held in 2014. Turnout was significantly lower in opposition districts, due in part to a decision to boycott the elections by the main opposition political societies and a lack of confidence among opposition communities in the electoral system. The government did not permit international election monitors. Domestic monitors generally concluded the authorities administered the elections without significant procedural irregularities. There were, however, broader concerns regarding voting-district boundaries.

Civilian authorities maintained effective control over the security forces.

The most serious human rights problems included limitations on citizens' ability to choose their government peacefully, including due to the government's ability to close arbitrarily or create registration difficulties for organized political societies; restrictions on free expression, assembly, and association; and lack of due process in the legal system, including arrests without warrants or charges and lengthy pretrial detentions--used especially in cases against opposition members and political or human rights activists. Beginning in June government action against the political opposition and civil society worsened these problems.

Other significant human rights problems included lack of judicial accountability for security officers accused by the government and nongovernmental organizations (NGOs) of committing human rights violations; defendants' lack of access to attorneys and ability to challenge evidence; prison overcrowding; violations of privacy; and other restrictions on civil liberties, including freedom of press and association. Societal discrimination continued against the Shia population, as did other forms of discrimination based on gender, religion, and nationality. The government imposed travel bans on political activists to prevent travel to participate in international fora. The government maintained the revocation of citizenship for 103 individuals whose citizenship it revoked in previous years, and it revoked citizenship from others during the year--including prominent Shia cleric Sheikh Isa Qassim, whose citizenship was revoked on June

20. There were reports of domestic violence against women and children. Despite government efforts at reform, the rights of foreign workers, particularly domestic workers, continued to be restricted, leaving them vulnerable to labor abuses and human trafficking.

Beginning in 2011 the country experienced a sustained period of unrest, including mass protests calling for political reform. The government has taken steps since then to implement recommendations by the Bahrain Independent Commission of Inquiry (BICI), which the government tasked to review widespread allegations of police brutality, torture, arrests, disappearances, and violence by both security forces and demonstrators that year. International and local human rights organizations viewed the BICI report as the standard against which to measure the country's human rights reforms and noted that the government had not fully implemented the report's recommendations, particularly those involving reconciliation, safeguarding freedom of expression, and accountability for abuses.

Section 1. Respect for the Integrity of the Person, Including Freedom from:

a. Arbitrary Deprivation of Life and other Unlawful or Politically Motivated Killings

There were some reports government security forces committed arbitrary or unlawful killings.

The Ministry of Interior Ombudsman's annual report detailed its investigations into seven detainee deaths that occurred from May 2015 to May. Investigators determined one prisoner died of a drug overdose, one committed suicide, four died from complications to preexisting medical conditions, and one died from injuries sustained when police attempted to arrest the individual. The government's investigations into the death of 17-year-old Ali Abdulghani during arrest and 35-year-old Hassan al-Hayki in police custody continued as of year's end (see section 1.c.).

Violent extremists perpetrated dozens of attacks against security officers and government officials during the year, killing one and injuring other security officers. On June 30, a remotely detonated bomb planted on Sitra highway near the village of Eker killed a woman and injured three of her children; no group claimed responsibility for the bombing.

b. Disappearance

There were no reports of politically motivated disappearances.

c. Torture and Other Cruel, Inhuman, or Degrading Treatment or Punishment

The constitution prohibits "harm[ing] an accused person physically or mentally." Some domestic and international human rights organizations, as well as former detainees, reported instances of torture, abuse, and other cruel, inhuman, or degrading treatment or punishment. Human rights groups reported prisoner accounts alleging security officials beat them, placed them in stress positions, humiliated them in front of other prisoners, deprived them of sleep and prayers, insulted them based on their religious beliefs, and subjected them to sexual harassment, including removal of clothing and threat of rape. Officials reportedly kept some detainees in solitary confinement, sometimes in extreme temperatures; poured cold water on them; and forced them to stand for long periods. Human rights organizations also reported authorities prevented some detainees from using toilet facilities, withheld food and drink, and denied medical treatment to injured or ill detainees and prisoners. Detainees also reported that security forces committed some abuses during searches, arrests at private residences, and during transportation. Detainees reported intimidation took place at the Ministry of Interior's Criminal Investigation Directorate (CID). In a report based on an unannounced visit to Jaw Prison in November 2015, the Commission on Prisoner and Detainee Rights (PDRC) confirmed allegations that prison staff had physically assaulted prisoners. The ministry denied torture and abuse were systemic. The government reported it had equipped all interrogation rooms, including those at local police stations and the CID, with closed-circuit television cameras monitored at all times. The PDRC repeatedly noted in reports released 2014-16 that many facilities had areas without video monitoring.

Some detainees at the CID reported security officials used physical and psychological mistreatment to extract confessions and statements under duress or to inflict retribution and punishment. The PDRC made an unannounced visit to the CID in 2014 and found that officials kept some prisoners handcuffed for the duration of their time at the facility, provided food at irregular times, and restricted prisoner access to a single toilet. It has not been made public whether the PDRC visited the facility since 2014.

The Ministry of Interior's ombudsman reported it received 68 complaints against the CID and 65 against Jaw Prison from May 2015 to May. The ombudsman referred 28 of the cases against the CID and 23 against Jaw Prison for criminal or disciplinary procedures; 37 additional cases were still under investigation.

Human rights groups reported authorities subjected children, sometimes under the age of 15, to various forms of mistreatment, including beating, slapping, kicking, and verbal abuse. The age of majority in the country is 15 years old, and the law considers all persons over this age to be adults. Authorities held detainees under the age of 15 at the Juvenile Care Center. The Ministry of Interior reported police arrested 31 children under the age of 15 from January to September; as of September there was one child at the Juvenile Care Center awaiting trial and 11 more serving their sentences. The PDRC visited the CID in 2014 and found that staff was not trained to treat special needs suspects or to treat those between the ages of 15 and 18 differently than adults.

On April 4, 17-year-old Ali Abdulghani died in the hospital from head injuries sustained during his March 31 arrest in the village of Shahrakkan. The government reported that police pursued Abdulghani based on a five-year sentence he had received in his absence. During the pursuit the government claimed Abdulghani entered a building under construction and either fell or jumped to his death. Critics disputed the government's version of events and alleged a police car had intentionally hit Abdulghani. According to press reports, the ombudsman and Special Investigative Unit (SIU) investigated and determined police acted appropriately.

Prison and Detention Center Conditions

Human rights activists reported conditions in prisons and detention centers were harsh and sometimes life threatening due to overcrowding, physical abuse, and inadequate sanitary conditions and medical care. Detainees and human rights organizations also reported abuse in official pretrial detention centers, as well as in Jaw Prison and Dry Dock Detention Center.

Physical Conditions: Human rights organizations and prisoners reported gross overcrowding in detention facilities, which placed a strain on administration and led to a high prisoner-to-staff ratio. Observers reported that from 2013 to year's end, the Jaw Prison population increased, perhaps to as high as 3,600 at times, while the ombudsman reported the number of prison guards remained the same, at 23 for the day shift. In October 2015 the Ministry of Interior reported it had opened four new buildings at Jaw Prison during the year and transferred inmates under the age of 21 to new buildings for convicted youth at the Dry Dock facility.

PDRC reports from 2015 detailed concerns about prison conditions including overcrowding, unsanitary conditions, and lack of access to basic supplies. Human rights organizations noted their concern about the health of prisoners with chronic medical conditions, including cancer.

Social media estimated there were up to 400 school-age youth in prison. The ministry held detainees under the age of 15 at the Juvenile Care Center, which, according to a PDRC report, was under capacity at the time of the commission's unannounced visit in January 2015. As of June 2015, convicted males between the ages of 15 and 21 were housed in newly constructed buildings located on the grounds of the Dry Dock facility, but they were kept separate from pretrial detainees. The ministry separated prisoners under the age of 18 from those between the ages of 18 and 21. Upon reaching the age of 21, prisoners are transferred to the general population at Jaw Prison. In September 2015 the Royal Charity Organization opened a branch of the Nasser Center for Rehabilitation and Vocational Training at Jaw Prison with space for 50 inmates to participate; this program continued to operate.

The ombudsman's annual report detailed its investigations into the seven detainee deaths that occurred from May 2015 to May. Investigators determined one prisoner died of a drug overdose, one committed suicide, four died from complications to preexisting medical conditions, and one died from injuries sustained when police attempted to arrest the individual.

The ombudsman and the SIU also reported their investigations into the July 31 death of 35-year-old Hassan al-Hayki. Authorities announced he died of a heart attack shortly after arriving at a hospital from the Dry Dock pretrial detention facility; opposition activists alleged al-Hayki was mistreated following his arrest. Al-Hayki had been in custody since his July 13 arrest on suspicion of involvement in the June 30 bombing in Eker (see section 1.a.).

Although the government reported potable water was available for all detainees, and there were water coolers in all detention centers, there were reports of lack of access to water for drinking and washing, lack of shower facilities and soap, and unhygienic toilet facilities. There were also reports of air conditioning units not running in extremely hot weather. Human rights organizations reported food was adequate for most prisoners; however, those prisoners needing dietary accommodations due to medical conditions had difficulty receiving special dietary provisions. Other detainees reported physical abuse, verbal assault, and threats of sexual assault, as well as denial of sleep, prayer, and bathroom access.

There were no accommodations for persons with disabilities in prisons and detention centers. Human rights groups reported prisoners who became physically or mentally disabled while in custody relied on fellow prisoners for their care.

Prisoners needing medical attention reported difficulty in alerting guards to their needs, and medical clinics at the facilities were understaffed. Prisoners with chronic medical conditions including sickle-cell anemia, diabetes, and gout had difficulty accessing regular medical care. Those needing transportation to outside medical facilities reported delays in scheduling offsite treatment, especially those needing follow-up care for complex or chronic conditions. The PDRC noted numerous deficiencies with health services at most facilities. There were outbreaks of communicable diseases that spread quickly and severely, due to overcrowded conditions, lack of sanitation, and understaffed medical clinics.

In March 2015 hundreds of prisoners at Jaw Prison participated in a riot that caused significant damage to the prison and injured 245 inmates and police. The prison kept some prisoners in tents in the yard for up to three months after the riot, with limited access to showers. There were also reports authorities partially shaved prisoners' heads to humiliate them, placed them in stress positions, made them mimic animals, and beat them. Detainees reported police who abused them self-identified as Jordanian Special Police Force (known as the Darak). Prosecutors charged more than 50 inmates in connection with the rioting. Although authorities reported the SIU continued to investigate alleged abuse, as of years' end, it had not brought any disciplinary or criminal proceedings against police or security forces allegedly involved in abuses during and after the riot.

Administration: The Ministry of Interior reported authorities registered the location of detainees from the moment of arrest. Authorities generally allowed prisoners to file complaints to judicial authorities without censorship, and officials from the ombudsman were available to respond to complaints. Human rights groups, however, reported some prisoners faced reprisals from prison staff for lodging complaints. Prisoners had access to visitors at least once a month, often more frequently, and authorities permitted them 30 minutes of calls each week, although authorities reportedly denied prisoners communication with lawyers and family members at times. Authorities generally permitted prisoners to practice their religion, but there were reports authorities sometimes denied prisoners access to religious services and prayer time.

<u>Independent Monitoring</u>: Authorities permitted access for the quasi-governmental National Institution for Human Rights (NIHR) and PDRC, as well as the government's ombudsman and SIU. Some local and international human rights organizations expressed concern regarding the degree of independence of the domestic groups.

The SIU, formed in 2012, acted as a mechanism for the public to complain about prisoner mistreatment or conditions in prisons and detention facilities. The SIU reported it received 137 complaints through August, five of which it referred to court; the others remained under investigation. The ombudsman began monitoring prisons and detention centers in 2013, conducting announced and unannounced visits and accepting written and in-person complaints. From May 2015 until May, the office received 305 complaints and an additional 687 requests for assistance. The ombudsman had complaint boxes at most Ministry of Interior detention facilities and staffed a permanent office at Jaw Prison to receive complaints. The ombudsman reported it was able to get evidence preserved on more than one occasion after receiving a complaint about mistreatment.

In December 2015 the NIHR published its third annual report, which covered 2015. The NIHR reported it received 88 complaints representing 119 complainants for 2015 and an additional 124 requests for assistance and legal advice. Separately, the NIHR reported it visited Jaw prison and interviewed more than 40 prisoners, and it had followed complaints from inmates' families regarding alleged denial of medical treatment.

From the end of 2014 throughout the year, the PDRC conducted unannounced visits at a number of detention facilities, including Jaw Prison, the CID, Juvenile Care Center, Women's Detention Center, Women's Reformation and Rehabilitation Center, and four police directorates; it posted reports on these facilities on its website.

d. Arbitrary Arrest or Detention

The constitution prohibits arbitrary arrest and detention, although local and international human rights groups continued to report the practice of detaining individuals without notifying them at the time of the arrest of the legal authority of the person conducting the arrest, the reasons for the arrest, and the charges against them. Human rights groups claimed the Ministry of Interior conducted many arrests at private residences without either presenting an arrest warrant or presenting an inaccurate or incomplete one, but government sources disputed these claims.

In 2013 the king tightened penalties for those involved in terrorism, banned demonstrations in the capital, allowed for legal action against political associations accused of inciting and supporting violence and terrorism, and granted security services increased powers to protect society from terrorism, including the ability to declare a State of National Safety. Human rights groups asserted the 2013 laws conflicted with protections against arbitrary arrest and detention, including for freedom of speech.

In 2014 authorities detained leading opposition society Wifaq secretary general Sheikh Ali Salman over concerns about political statements. Authorities charged him with four crimes: inciting a change of government by force, inciting hatred of a segment of society, inciting others to break the law, and insulting the Ministry of Interior. In June 2015 a criminal court acquitted Salman of inciting political change by force but sentenced him to four years on the other three charges. Both Salman and the prosecution appealed. On May 30, the appeals court convicted him on all charges, including the one on which the lower court had acquitted him, and sentenced him to nine years in prison. In October the Court of Cassation threw out the appeals court decision and sent the case back to have another appeals court review the case. At that review on December 12, the appeals court reinstated Salman's nine-year sentence; Salman remained in custody at Jaw Prison at year's end. His legal team claimed the prosecution entered falsified evidence, including altered transcripts of speeches, and that prison officials had prevented the team from passing legal documents to Salman, complicating their ability to mount a defense. Evidence presented against Salman in court consisted solely of public statements he made in sermons or speeches. In November 2015 the UN working group on arbitrary detention determined that authorities had arbitrarily detained Salman. On September 15, police questioned Salman at the CID in connection with a letter submitted with his name to the UN high commissioner for human rights, Zeid Ra'ad al-Hussein (see section 5), but as of year's end, no new charges have been filed.

Role of the Police and Security Apparatus

The Ministry of Interior is responsible for internal security and controls the public security force and specialized security units responsible for maintaining internal order. The coast guard is also under its jurisdiction. The Bahrain Defense Force is primarily responsible for defending against external threats, while the Bahrain

National Guard is responsible for both external and internal threats. Security forces effectively maintained order and generally responded in a measured way to violent attacks.

Civilian authorities maintained effective control over security forces during the year, although impunity remained a problem. In 2012 the government established the SIU to investigate and refer cases of security force misconduct to the appropriate court, which includes civilian criminal courts, the ministry's Military Court, and administrative courts. As of August the SIU reported it had received and investigated 137 new complaints since the beginning of the year. The SIU submitted five of these cases, with a total of 11 defendants, to civilian criminal court, and had one officer and two enlisted men convicted, with one sentenced to a year in prison. The SIU also referred some cases to the ministry's administrative and military courts. As of September the ministry reported 41 police officers were in jail, another nine were in detention awaiting trial, and 190 had received reprimands. The ministry generally did not release the names of officers convicted, demoted, reassigned, or fired for misconduct. Many human rights groups asserted that investigations into police abuse were slow and ineffective.

Unidentified individuals conducted numerous attacks aimed at security personal during the year, which the perpetrators often filmed and posted to social media. These videos showed attackers using Molotov cocktails and other improvised weapons against police patrols and stations, including in close proximity to bystanders. Police avoided responding with deadly force.

In 2012 the king ordered the creation of the Bahrain National Security Agency's (BNSA) Office for the Inspector General and the Ministry of Interior Ombudsman. While both offices were responsible for addressing cases of mistreatment and abuse, there was little public information available about the BNSA inspector general's activities.

In 2012 the minister of interior approved a new police code of conduct that requires officers to abide by 10 principles, including limited use of force and zero tolerance for torture and mistreatment. According to government officials, the code forbids the use of force "except when absolutely necessary." The Royal Police Academy included the code in its curriculum in 2012 and provided new recruits with copies in English and Arabic. The ministry reported it took disciplinary action against officers who did not comply with the code.

The Ombudsman maintained a hotline for citizens to report police abuse, but human rights groups reported many citizens hesitated to report abuse for fear of retribution. As of September, the police hotline had received 260 calls. The Ombudsman reported a reduction in the number of complaints it received about the riot police from 15 in the 2014-2015 reporting cycle to two in 2015-2016.

Local activists and human rights organizations claimed that the demographics of the police and security forces were not representative of Bahrain's communities. To address these concerns and in response to a BICI recommendation on integrating Shia citizens into the police force, the government established the community police program, which recruits individuals to work in their own neighborhoods, in 2012. In 2012, the government graduated 577 new police from its academy and said that the majority would be "working in the community." In October 2015, the government reported 504 community police officers graduated from the same community policing program in 2015, bringing the total number of community police that have graduated from the Royal Police Academy to 1500. As of September, the government reported it had not hired any additional community police in 2016, leaving the total number of community police at approximately 1,400, of which 320 were women. Community members have confirmed that Shia have been among those integrated into the community police and the police cadets, but not in significant numbers; information is not available on recruitment rates of Shia into other security forces.

Arrest Procedures and Treatment of Detainees

The law stipulates law enforcement officials may arrest individuals without a warrant only if they are caught committing certain crimes for which there is sufficient evidence to press charges. Local activists reported police sometimes made arrests without presenting a warrant.

By law the arresting authority must interrogate an arrested individual immediately and cannot detain the person for more than 48 hours, after which authorities must either release the detainee or transfer the person to the Public Prosecution Office (PPO) for further questioning. The PPO is required to question the detainee within 24 hours, and the detainee has the right to legal counsel during questioning. To hold the detainee longer, the PPO must issue a formal detention order based on the charges against the detainee. Authorities may extend detention up to seven days for further questioning. If authorities require any further extension, they must bring the detainee before a judge, who may authorize a further extension not exceeding 45 days. The High Criminal Court must authorize any extensions beyond that period and any renewals at 45-day intervals. In the case of alleged acts of terror, law enforcement officials may detain individuals for questioning for an initial five days, which the PPO can extend up to 60 days. A functioning system of bail provides maximum and minimum bail amounts based on the charges; however, judges often denied bail requests without explanation, even in nonviolent cases. The bail law allows the presiding judge to determine the amount within these parameters on a case-by-case basis.

Attorneys reported difficulty in gaining access to their clients in a timely manner through all stages of the legal process, including reports defense attorneys had difficulty registering themselves as a detainee's legal representative because of arbitrary bureaucratic hurdles, had their qualifications arbitrarily questioned by police, were not notified of their client's location in custody, were directed to seek a court order to meet with their client, were prohibited from meeting their client in private, were prohibited from passing legal documents to their client, were told at short notice when their client would be questioned by the PPO, were not allowed to be present during questioning by police or prosecutor, and were not provided access or allowed to consult with their clients in court. While the state provides counsel to indigent detainees, there were reports detainees never met with their state appointed attorney before or during their trial.

According to reports by local and international human rights groups, authorities held some detainees for weeks with limited access to outside resources. The government sometimes withheld information from detainees and their families about the detainees' whereabouts for days.

On October 24, Sayed Alawi Hussain Alawi from Diraz went missing, and his family filed a missing person's report with police that night. The family then received a call from an individual who identified himself as being from the CID, who said police had arrested Alawi. According to social media reports, police prevented Alawi's lawyer from meeting with his client and prevented Alawi from calling his family until December 1.

In August 2015 authorities arrested former opposition member of parliament, Sheikh Hassan Isa, at the airport upon his return from abroad. According to Wifaq CID investigators prohibited Isa's lawyers from speaking to him and from being present during his questioning. Authorities allowed Isa to meet with his lawyers only after the lawyers filed multiple requests. As of year's end, his trial continued.

<u>Arbitrary Arrest</u>: Human rights groups reported the Ministry of Interior sometimes arrested individuals for activities such as calling for and attending protests and demonstrations, expressing their opinion either in public or on social media, and associating with persons of interest to law enforcement. Some of these detained individuals reported arresting forces did not show them warrants. Authorities arrested dozens of participants in a nonviolent, long-term sit-in protesting the revocation of Sheikh Isa Qassim's citizenship outside of his residence in Diraz (see Section 2.b., Freedom of Assembly). The government maintained that police only summoned, questioned, and detained individuals who had broken the law.

In July 2015 police summoned former president of the capital governorate's municipal council, Majeed Milad, to the Houra Police Station and arrested him. A criminal court found him guilty of "incitement of hatred against the regime," during a speech he gave at a Ramadan gathering, and gave him a one-year sentence. Authorities released him from prison on July 1. (See section 2.a, for information about the arrest and detention of human rights activist Nabeel Rajab.)

<u>Detainee's Ability to Challenge Lawfulness of Detention before a Court</u>: The constitution prohibits arbitrary arrest and detention, although local and international human rights groups continued to report the practice of detaining individuals without notifying them at the time of the arrest of the legal authority of the person conducting the arrest, the reasons for the arrest, and the charges against them. There were reports that authorities sometimes delayed or limited an individual's access to an attorney. There were no reports of courts finding individuals to have been unlawfully detained and recommending compensation.

e. Denial of Fair Public Trial

Although the constitution provides for an independent judiciary, the judiciary remained vulnerable to political pressures, especially in cases involving political opposition figures. The judiciary has two branches: the civil law courts deal with all commercial, civil, and criminal cases, including family issues of non-Muslims, and the sharia law courts handle personal status cases of Muslims. The government subdivided the sharia courts into Sunni and Shia sharia courts. Many of the country's approximately 160 judges were foreign judges serving on limited-term contracts (which are subject to government approval for renewal and residence in the country). The Supreme Judicial Council is responsible for supervising the work of the courts, including judges, and the PPO.

Trial Procedures

The constitution presumes defendants are innocent until proven guilty. By law authorities should inform detainees of the charges against them upon arrest. Civil and criminal trial procedures provide for a public trial. A panel of three judges makes the rulings. Defendants have the right to consultation with an attorney of their choice within 48 hours (unless the government charges them pursuant to counterterrorism legislation); however, there are reports that defendants and their lawyers have had difficulty getting police, public prosecutor, and courts to recognize or register representation by an attorney. The government provides counsel at public expense to indigent defendants. No law governs defendants' access to government-held evidence, and such evidence was available at the discretion of the court. Defendants have the right to present witnesses and evidence on their behalf. While defendants have the right to question witnesses against them, the judges can declare the questions to be irrelevant and prohibit a line of questioning without providing reasoning. Prosecutors rarely present evidence orally in court but provide it in written and digital formats to judges in their chambers. In criminal trials prosecutors and judges walk into the courtroom together. Defendants are not compelled to testify or to confess guilt and have the right to appeal. The government frequently tries defendants in their absence.

Family status law varied according to Shia or Sunni interpretations of Islamic law, especially for women (see section 6).

Political Prisoners and Detainees

The government denied holding any political prisoners, although it acknowledged holding several dozen high-profile individuals, including leaders or prominent members of political societies and organizations and others who were publically critical of government institutions or government actions prior to their arrests. Human rights organizations and opposition groups asserted there were more than 4,000 political prisoners in the country, but this number could not be confirmed. According to the PDRC, the total number of individuals in custody charged with all types of crimes is 3,700 and includes 700 foreigners. Authorities held some high-profile prisoners separately from the general prison population. Activist Nabeel Rajab remained in detention as the only prisoner held at the East Riffa Police Station, and human rights organizations raised concerns that he was not consistently provided prompt access to medical care (see section 2.a.). There were some reports authorities held political prisoners in better conditions compared to other prisoners and detainees.

In March 2015 the Ministry of Interior arrested Fadhel Abbas, secretary general of the Democratic Unity Gathering Society (al-Wahdawi), in relation to a tweet sent by the al-Wahdawi political society that criticized the country's military involvement in Yemen. A criminal court sentenced him in June 2015 to five years in prison for "spreading false information that could harm the military operations of Bahrain and its allies." On October 27, an appeals court reduced his sentence to three years, and at year's end he remained in Jaw Prison.

Authorities released several prominent politicians and activists arrested in 2011 from prison at the completion of their prescribed sentences, including Mohammed Ali al-Mahfoodh on April 30, Mahdi Abu Deeb on April 1, and Salah al-Khawaja on March 19. In June 2015 authorities pardoned and released former Wa'ad secretary general Ibrahim Sharif, but police rearrested him on new charges 23 days later, and he spent another year in jail (see section 2.a.).

(See section 1.d. for information about the arrest and detention of Wifaq secretary general Sheikh Ali Salman. See section 2.a. for more information about the arrest and detention of activists Nabeel Rajab and Zainab al-Khawaja.)

Civil Judicial Procedures and Remedies

Citizens may bring civil suits before a court seeking cessation of or damages for some types of human rights violations. In many such situations, however, the law prevents citizens from filing civil suits against security agencies.

f. Arbitrary or Unlawful Interference with Privacy, Family, Home, or Correspondence

Although the constitution prohibits such actions, the government violated prohibitions against interference with privacy, family, home, or correspondence. Human rights organizations reported security forces sometimes entered homes without authorization and destroyed or confiscated personal property. The law requires the government to obtain a court order before monitoring telephone calls, e-mail, and personal correspondence. Many citizens and human rights organizations believed police used informer networks, including ones that targeted or used children under 18 years of age.

Reports also indicated the government used computer programs to spy on political activists and members of the opposition inside and outside the country.

According to local and international human rights groups, security officials sometimes threatened detainees' family members with reprisals for the detainee's unwillingness to cooperate during interrogations and refusal to sign confession statements.

Section 2. Respect for Civil Liberties, Including:

a. Freedom of Speech and Press

The constitution provides for freedom of speech and press, "provided that the fundamental beliefs of Islamic doctrine are not infringed, the unity of the people is not prejudiced, and discord and sectarianism are not aroused." In practice the government limited freedom of speech and press through active prosecution of individuals under libel, slander, and national security laws that targeted civilian and professional journalists and by passing legislation to limit speech in print and social media.

Freedom of Speech and Expression: The law forbids any speech that infringes on public order or morals. While individuals openly expressed critical opinions regarding domestic political and social issues in private settings, those who publicly expressed such opinions often faced repercussions. During the year the government took steps against what it considered acts of civil disobedience, which included critical speech, under charges of unlawful assembly or "insulting the king." A 2014 amendment to the penal code increased penalties to no less than one year and no more than seven years in prison, plus a fine, for anyone who "offends the monarch of the Kingdom of Bahrain, the flag, or the national emblem."

On June 13, police arrested Bahrain Center for Human Rights (BCHR) president Nabeel Rajab for tweets released in April 2015 criticizing Saudi-led coalition's military operations in Yemen and treatment of prisoners in Jaw Prison. Police initially arrested Rajab on these charges in April 2015 but released him from prison in July 2015 when he received a pardon in connection with a previous arrest. Rajab's trial on the latter charges began in July and continued as of year's end. At his hearing on December 28, the judge ordered Rajab released on bail; however, on the same day, the public prosecutor announced that Rajab would remain in detention under investigation on separate charges stemming from "publishing false news and statements" for statements in a *New York Times* op-ed published in Rajab's name on September 4 and another article attributed to Rajab that was published in the French newspaper *Le Monde* on December 19. That case had not gone to trial as of year's end, and Rajab remained in custody.

In July 2015 authorities arrested Ibrahim Sharif after he delivered a speech calling for reforms and making reference to the "embers of revolution." This arrest came 23 days after the king pardoned him for a conviction stemming from involvement in the 2011 unrest, for which Sharif had spent more than four years in prison. In the 2015 case, the prosecutor charged Sharif with "promoting political change through forceful means." On February 24, a criminal court found him guilty of "inciting hatred against the regime" and sentenced him to one year in jail. The authorities released him on July 11. On November 7, the appeals process concluded with no additional jail time for Sharif, although a travel ban remained in effect at year's end. Authorities also brought charges of "inciting hatred and contempt against the regime" against Sharif on November 13 after he gave an interview to the Associated Press in which he said that the November visit by United Kingdom Prince Charles and wife Camilla could "whitewash" the ongoing crackdown on dissent. Sharif was not taken into police custody, and the charges were dropped on November 24.

On June 21, an appeals court upheld a one-year jail sentence against women's rights activist Ghada Jamsheer in conjunction with a series of tweets about corruption at a local hospital and a physical altercation that happened when she was in pretrial detention in 2014. Authorities arrested Jamsheer on August 15 when she returned from a trip abroad. She was released from prison on December 14 under the agreement that she would perform community service in lieu of serving the remaining time on her sentence.

On February 2, an appeals court upheld a nine-month sentence issued against activist Zainab al-Khawaja in June 2015 for trespassing. In October 2015 a different appeals court reduced a separate sentence against her for tearing up a picture of the king in court from three years to one year. Al-Khawaja claimed she tore up the picture as a political statement, while the government maintained the charge against her was for contempt of court. Police took al-Khawaja into custody on March 14 to serve these two sentences, but authorities released her on May 31 for "humanitarian reasons" after she served 2.5 months of her 21-month sentence. She subsequently left the country and at year's end remained abroad.

<u>Press and Media Freedoms</u>: The government did not own any print media, but the Ministry of Information Affairs and other government entities exercised considerable control over privately owned domestic print media.

The government owned and operated all domestic radio and television stations. Audiences generally received radio and television broadcasts in Arabic, Farsi, and English from countries in the region, including by satellite, without interference. The ministry reviewed all books and publications prior to issuing printing licenses. The Ministry of Justice and Islamic Affairs reviewed books that discussed religion.

The Ministry of Information Affairs did not renew the accreditation of three journalists who worked for international media agencies, Nazeha Saeed, Reem Khalifa, and Hasan Jamali. The ministry did not give reason for its decision, nor was recourse available. It brought criminal complaints against journalists who continued to work without accreditation.

<u>Violence and Harassment</u>: According to local journalists, authorities harassed, arrested, or threatened journalists and photographers due to their reporting. Authorities claimed, however, that some individuals who identified themselves as journalists and photographers associated with violent opposition groups and produced propaganda and recruiting videos for these groups. International media representatives reported difficulty in obtaining visas to work as journalists. The government arrested or deported individuals who were in the country on other types of visas and who engaged in even limited journalistic activities. The government sentenced several journalists and bloggers arrested in 2015-16 to prison for social media postings.

<u>Censorship or Content Restrictions</u>: Government censorship occurred. Ministry of Information Affairs personnel actively monitored and blocked stories on matters deemed sensitive, especially those related to sectarianism, national security, or criticism of the royal family, the Saudi royal family, or the judiciary. Journalists widely practiced self-censorship. Some members of media reported government officials contacted editors directly and told them to stop writing about certain subjects or told them not to publish a press release or story.

The press and publications law prohibits anti-Islamic content in media and mandates imprisonment for "exposing the state's official religion for offense and criticism." The law states, "any publication that prejudices the ruling system of the country and its official religion can be banned from publication by a ministerial order."

Index on Censorship, an international NGO that supports freedom of expression, reported the ministry's Press and Publications Directorate banned and confiscated all copies of the book, *Political Organizations and Societies in Bahrain*, coauthored by Bahraini writer Abbas al-Murshid, and another book by al-Murshid, *Bahrain in the Gulf Gazetteer*. Additionally, a number of books remained banned from 2010, including the Arabic translation of *The Personal Diary of Charles Belgrave* and *Unbridled Hatreds: Reading in the Fate of Ancient Hatreds*, by Bahraini author Nader Kadim.

Libel/Slander Laws: The government enforced libel and national security-related laws restricting freedom of the press. The penal code prohibits libel, slander, and "divulging secrets"; and it stipulates a punishment of imprisonment for no more than two years or a fine of no more than 200 dinars ($540). Application of the slander law was selective.

National Security: National security-related law provides for fines of as much as 10,000 dinars ($27,000) and prison sentences of at least six months for criticizing the king or inciting actions that undermine state security, as well as fines of up to 2,000 dinars ($5,400) for 14 related offenses. Punishable activities include publicizing statements issued by a foreign state or organization before obtaining ministry approval, publishing any reports that may adversely affect the dinar's value, reporting any offense against a head of a state that maintains diplomatic relations with the country, and publishing offensive remarks about an accredited representative of a foreign country due to acts connected with the person's position.

Internet Freedom

More than 90 percent of citizens had access to the internet. The government restricted internet freedom and monitored individuals' online activities, including via social media, leading to degradation of internet and mobile phone services for some neighborhoods and to legal action against some internet users.

On January 4, police arrested optometrist, Dr. Saeed al-Samahiji, for tweets critical of Saudi Arabia's execution of Shia cleric and political activist Nimr al-Nimr. On April 7, a criminal court sentenced him to a one-year prison term for "insulting a neighboring country." The appeals court upheld the conviction on September 7. He remained in Jaw Prison at year's end.

Three days after a sit-in outside of Sheikh Isa Qassim's house in Diraz began in late June, residents complained that mobile phone networks and internet services were significantly reduced each evening. The offshore-based Bahrain Watch organization concluded two of the three main Internet Service Providers in the country deliberately restricted access for some users each day during certain times.

In 2013 the Ministry of Communication blocked 70 websites in accordance with laws passed following parliament's recommendations. The government stated that it took this action to prevent access to "terrorist materials," but NGOs asserted many of the websites featured only political speech. As of year's end, the websites were intermittently accessible.

Academic Freedom and Cultural Events

The government restricted academic freedom and cultural events. Some academics engaged in self-censorship, avoiding discussion of contentious political issues.

Human rights advocates claimed government officials unfairly distributed university scholarships and were biased against Shia, for both political and religious reasons, when admitting students into certain programs. In 2011 the government instituted interviews into the university selection process, partially to correct for grade inflation, as there is no national standardized test to account for different grading practices across secondary schools; however, students reported authorities asked them about their and their families' political beliefs as part of the interviews. The government maintained it distributed all scholarships and made all placements based on merit.

b. Freedom of Peaceful Assembly and Association

Freedom of Assembly

The constitution provides for the right of free assembly, but the law restricts the exercise of this right. The government limited and controlled political gatherings and denied permits for organized demonstrations. For the second year, there were no authorized demonstrations, although the Ministry of Interior generally did not intervene in peaceful, unauthorized demonstrations. The ministry reported it did not approve any major demonstrations during the year due to past failures by organizers to control their own events. Political societies, however, reported the ministry refused even to accept permit requests, whether delivered by hand, by registered post, or by fax. The opposition group Wifaq reported that despite many new requests, its last approval for a march came in 2014.

According to the Ministry of Interior, three persons from the locality where an event will take place must submit a signed request to the chief of public security three days in advance, to receive permission to hold a public gathering. The law outlines the locations and times during which it prohibits functions, including areas close to hospitals, airports, commercial locations, security-related facilities, and downtown Manama. In addition to the locations listed in the law, the chief of public security may change the time, place, or route of the event if there is a possibility that it would cause a breach of public order. The law states mourners may not turn funeral processions into political rallies, and that security officials may be present at any public gathering.

The law states every public gathering shall have a committee consisting of a head and at least two members. The committee is responsible for supervising and preventing any illegal acts during the function. According to the law, the Ministry of Interior is not obligated to justify why it approves or denies requests to allow protests. The penal code penalizes any gathering "of five or more individuals" that is held for the "purpose of committing crimes or inciting others to commit crimes." Lawyers asserted authorities should not prevent demonstrations in advance based on assumptions crimes would be committed. Authorities prohibited the use of vehicles in any demonstration, protest, or gathering unless organizers obtained special written permission from the head of public security.

Organizers of an unauthorized gathering faced prison sentences of three to six months. The minimum sentence for participating in an illegal gathering is one month, and the maximum is two years. Authorities gave longer sentences for cases where demonstrators used violence in an illegal gathering. The maximum fine is 200 dinars ($540). The law regulates election campaigning and prohibits political activities at worship centers, universities, schools, government buildings, and public institutions. The government did not allow individuals to use mosques, maatams (Shia religious community centers), or other religious sites for political gatherings. During the year authorities questioned and detained some political society officials for discussing political matters in religious venues.

Police arrested or summoned several dozen individuals, including Shia clerics, in relation to their alleged participation in the Diraz sit-in, which began June 20 following the revocation of Sheikh Isa Qassim's citizenship. On July 30, police arrested Shia cleric Sheikh Sayed Majeed al-Mashaal, head of the banned Islamic Ulema Council, on allegations he participated on June 30 in the sit-in. On August 31, a court sentenced al-Mashaal to two years in prison on these charges and transferred him to Jaw Prison. On December 1, an appeals court reduced an additional one-year sentence he received on October 7 on other charges stemming from his participation in the sit-in on July 19.

Freedom of Association

The constitution provides for freedom of association, but the government limited this right. The government required all groups to register: civil society groups with the Ministry of Social Development, political societies with the Ministry of Justice and Islamic Affairs, and labor unions with the Ministry of Labor. The government decided whether a group was social or political in nature, based on its proposed bylaws. The law prohibits any activity by an unlicensed society, as well as any political activity by a licensed civil society group. A number of unlicensed societies were active in the country (see also section 3).

A civil society group applying for registration must submit its bylaws signed by all founding members, together with minutes of the founding committee's meetings containing the names, professions, places of residence, and signatures of all founding members. The law grants the Ministry of Social Development the right to reject the registration of any civil society group if it finds the society's services unnecessary, already provided by another society, contrary to state security, or aimed at reviving a previously dissolved society. Associations whose applications the authorities rejected or ignored may appeal to the High Civil Court, which may annul the ministry's decision or refuse the appeal.

Many NGOs and civil society activists asserted the Ministry of Social Development routinely exploited its oversight role to stymie the activities of NGOs and other civil society organizations. While some local NGOs asserted bureaucratic incompetence characterized the ministry's dealings with NGOs, many others stated officials actively sought to undermine some groups' activities and imposed burdensome bureaucratic procedures on NGO board members and volunteers. The Ministries of Justice and Interior must vet funding from international sources, and authorities sometimes did not authorize it.

(For information on the closure of the Wifaq political society, see section 3, Political Parties and Political Participation.)

c. Freedom of Religion

See the Department of State's *International Religious Freedom Report* at www.state.gov/religiousfreedomreport/.

d. Freedom of Movement, Internally Displaced Persons, Protection of Refugees, and Stateless Persons

The constitution provides for freedom of internal movement, foreign travel, emigration, and repatriation. The government did not always respect these rights.

The government generally cooperated with the Office of the UN High Commissioner for Refugees (UNHCR) and other humanitarian organizations in providing protection and assistance to internally displaced persons, refugees, returning refugees, asylum seekers, stateless persons, or other persons of concern.

<u>Foreign Travel</u>: The law provides the government may reject for "reasonable cause" applications to obtain or renew passports, but the applicant has the right to appeal such decisions before the High Civil Court. Individuals, including citizens of other countries, reported authorities banned them from travel out of the country due to unpaid debt obligations or other fiduciary responsibilities with private individuals or with lending institutions. The government launched an online website during the year that allowed individuals to check their status before they traveled. Authorities relied on determinations of "national security" when adjudicating passport applications. During the year the authorities prevented a number of activists from leaving the country without providing options for legal recourse.

Starting in June approximately 40 individuals, including activists and opposition figures, reported customs agents stopped them from leaving the country. Individuals reportedly under "travel bans" claimed the government had not informed them of the ban, provided them with an official document citing the reason, or allowed them to present an appeal. In November police summoned some of these individuals to question them regarding allegations they participated in the Diraz sit-in. Critics alleged the authorities tried to build cases against the individuals retroactively to give the travel bans the appearance of legality. Observers noted the travel bans prevented activists from participating in UN Human Rights Council (HRC) sessions and other international events. In July the NIHR urged the government to stop issuing travel bans without a judicial order.

On November 10, authorities charged human rights lawyer, Mohamed al-Tajer, with insulting government institutions, inciting hatred of a religious sect, and misusing a telecommunications device, in part based on statements critical of the government that he made on a social media network. Al-Tajer had been banned from travel to the June HRC session. He was not detained, and the case had not gone to trial as of year's end.

Exile: There were no reports the government prohibited the return of individuals whom the government maintained were Bahraini citizens. The government, however, prohibited the return of those whose citizenship it formally revoked, or those it no longer considered citizens. There were reports of individuals who lived in self-imposed exile, often to avoid jail time for convictions imposed in their absence.

Citizenship: As a punitive measure, the government continued to revoke citizenship for both criminal and political cases. The minister of interior may also request that the cabinet approve revoking citizenship from a naturalized citizen who has violated specific conditions. The government has not implemented a comprehensive legal review process concerning citizen revocation, as recommended by the NIHR in 2015, to assure the government protected the rights of individuals and their family members. The government did not consider whether individuals may become stateless by these actions and has at times threatened to halt payments of pensions, or remove families from government-assisted housing if a head-of-household loses his citizenship. Some family members, especially females and minor children, reported difficulties renewing their passports and residence cards and obtaining birth certificates for children. During the year the government issued a number of individuals, whose citizenship it had revoked, limited validity Bahraini passports and deported them to Iraq, Iran, and Lebanon. There is no procedure for accused persons to mount a defense prior to having their citizenship revoked.

On June 20, the Bahrain News Agency (BNA) announced the government had revoked Shia cleric Sheikh Isa Qassim's citizenship. Government sources reported Qassim had the right to appeal the decision, but he declined to do so. On that same day, authorities raided his offices and froze his bank accounts. Authorities indicted him and two staff, Mirza al-Dirazi and Sheikh Hussain al-Mahrous, on money laundering charges citing large transfers of funds overseas that allegedly bypassed banks to avoid detection. Qassim denied the charges and has not attended any court proceedings. His supporters claimed the government targeted Qassim because of his status in the Shia community and asserted Qassim's office collected the funds and spent them according to Shia customs and obligations. As of December Qassim remained at his home in the village of Diraz. Supporters maintained a sit-in/vigil outside of his house in response to fears police would arrest him. Security forces have limited entrance into and egress out of the village to Diraz residents.

In January 2015 the BNA named 72 individuals who had their citizenship revoked but did not specify what violation each committed. The BNA instead provided a list of violations that may have led the authorities to act, including defaming the image of the regime and defaming brotherly countries. Authorities did not notify these individuals, who learned about the decision from the press. Some of the individuals had previously been involved in activism or in the political opposition. During the year the authorities gave at least three of these individuals limited validity passports and immediately deported them, including Sheikh Mohammed Khojasta on February 22, Hussein KhairAllah Mahood on February 24, and Masaud Jahromi on March 7.

In 2014 the Interior Ministry's Nationality, Passports, and Residence Directorate summoned 10 Bahrainis, whose citizenship the government revoked for politically motivated reasons in 2012 and against whom it filed criminal lawsuits, requesting them to defend their legal status and indicate whether they had found other citizens willing to sponsor them. Later in 2014, a court found them guilty of being in the country without sponsors and fined each 100 dinars ($270). Their appeal hearing continued in December 2015. On April 17, they lost their appeal. Authorities deported Taimoor Karimi to Iraq on June 26. Human rights organizations reported the remaining nine were at risk to be deported.

In 2014 a court adjourned an appeal brought by Ibrahim Karimi, who filed a constitutional challenge to his citizenship revocation--the only one to do so among the 31 whose citizenship was revoked in 2012. In September 2015 authorities arrested him on new charges related to social media postings and searched his house; authorities also again charged him with living in the country illegally. His trial on the new charges began January 31, and on March 31, he was sentenced to two years in prison. His appeal continued at year's end. Separately, on March 8, the appeals court upheld the original deportation order against him, putting him at risk of deportation once he completes his current sentence.

Protection of Refugees

<u>Access to Asylum</u>: The law does not provide for the granting of asylum or refugee status, and the government has not established a system for providing protection to refugees. The government at times provided protection against the expulsion or return of refugees to countries where their lives or freedom would be threatened on

account of their race, religion, nationality, membership in a particular social group, or political opinion; however, this was mostly limited to those who had been able to obtain and maintain employment in the country. Such individuals generally had access to health care and education services while employed but were at risk of being deported if they became unemployed or if their country of origin revoked their passports. The foreign minister told media in September 2015 that Bahrain had accepted "thousands" of Syrian refugees; however, UNHCR reported that as of June, there were 355 refugees registered with the agency.

Stateless Persons

Individuals generally derive citizenship from the father, but the king may confer or revoke it. Since the government only considers the father's citizenship when determining citizenship, it does not grant children born to a non-Bahraini father citizenship, even if they were born in Bahrain to a Bahraini mother. Likewise, the government does not provide a path to citizenship for foreign men married to Bahraini women, unlike the process by which foreign women married to Bahraini men may become citizens. Human rights organizations reported that these laws have resulted in stateless children, particularly when the foreign father is unable or unwilling to pursue citizenship from his country of origin for his children, or when the father himself was stateless, deceased, or unknown. It was unknown how many stateless persons resided in the country. Stateless persons had limited access to social services, education, and employment. There were reports authorities refused applications for birth certificates and passports for children whose Bahraini fathers were in prison because the fathers were not able to submit the applications in person (see section 6, Children).

The government charged individuals whose citizenship it revoked with violating immigration law.

Section 3. Freedom to Participate in the Political Process

Citizens have limited ability to choose their government and their political system. The constitution provides for a democratically elected Council of Representatives, the lower house of parliament. A constitutional amendment ratified in 2012 permits the king to dissolve the Council of Representatives, but it requires that he first consult the presidents of the upper and lower houses of parliament as well as the head of the Constitutional Court. The king also has the power to amend the constitution and to propose, ratify, and promulgate laws.

Elections and Political Participation

<u>Recent Elections</u>: Approximately 52 percent of eligible voters participated in parliamentary elections held in November 2014. Turnout was significantly lower in opposition districts, due to a decision to boycott by the main opposition political societies, who expressed a lack of confidence that the elections would produce a parliament that they believed would address their concerns in a fully representative way. Among these concerns the opposition contended the government delineated voter districts to provide for its desired electoral outcomes and marginalize opposition-majority districts. Prior to the election, in January 2014 the government relaunched the National Dialogue, which served as a forum for the government, legislature, and political societies to discuss political solutions to such issues, but it ended eight months later with little progress.

The government did not permit international election monitors. Domestic monitors generally concluded that authorities administered the elections without significant irregularities. There were, however, broader concerns regarding voting district boundaries and limitations on freedom of expression and association.

Violent oppositionists intimidated candidates, including through arson attacks on their personal property and businesses. Boycotters pressured other candidates to withdraw from the race.

<u>Political Parties and Political Participation</u>: The government did not allow the formation of political parties, but more than a dozen "political societies" developed political platforms, held internal elections, and hosted political gatherings. To apply for registration, a political society must submit its bylaws signed by all founding members, a list of all members and copies of their residency cards, and a financial statement identifying the society's sources of funding and bank information. The society's principles, goals, and programs must not run counter to sharia or national interest, as interpreted by the judiciary, nor may the society base itself on sectarian, geographic, or class identity. A number of societies operated outside of these rules, and some functioned on a sectarian basis.

The government authorized registered political societies to run candidates for office and to participate in other political activities. On May 22, parliament passed an amendment to the political societies' law, which banned serving clerics from membership in political societies (including in leadership positions) and involvement in political activities, even on a voluntary basis.

In 2013 the justice minister issued an order stipulating political societies should coordinate their contacts with foreign diplomatic or consular missions, foreign governmental organizations, or representatives of foreign governments with the Ministry of Foreign Affairs, which can elect to send a representative to the meeting. In 2014 the government actively enforced the order when it summoned two leaders of Wifaq for questioning for meeting a visiting foreign official without seeking government permission. There were no further reports of government enforcing this order.

On June 14, the Ministry of Justice filed a motion against the Wifaq political society, requesting the administrative court issue an emergency order to shut down the group and accusing the society of creating "an environment for terrorism, extremism, and violence." The judge agreed to the immediate suspension of Wifaq's activities. Authorities sealed Wifaq's buildings, removed its signs, froze its bank accounts, and blocked its website. Days later, the ministry announced an additional motion to dissolve Wifaq on an expedited basis. On June 28, judges denied Wifaq's legal team access to records at its headquarters and additional time to prepare its defense. Wifaq's lawyers resigned in protest, but the case continued before the court. On July 17, the judges formally ordered Wifaq closed and its assets seized, which the administrative appeals court upheld on September 22. On October 26, the ministry announced it would auction off items seized from Wifaq's headquarters on November 7; but it then put the auction on hold when Wifaq appealed the case to the Court of Cassation on October 30. As of year's end, the Court of Cassation had not set a date for the hearing.

Individuals active with opposition political society groups also faced repercussions during the year (see section 1.e., Political Prisoners).

<u>Participation of Women and Minorities</u>: The 2014 elections selected three women to parliament's 40-member lower elected house. Also in 2014 the royal court appointed nine women to the Shura Council, the appointed 40-member upper house, and the prime minister appointed a woman to the 26-seat cabinet. During the year the government appointed two additional women as judges, bringing the total to eight. There were also five female prosecutors.

Shia and Sunni citizens have equal rights before the law, but Sunnis dominated political life, while the majority of citizens are Shia. The 2014 elections brought 13 Shia members to parliament. The appointed Shura Council included 17 Shia members, one Jewish member, and one Christian member. Five of the 26 appointed cabinet ministers were Shia, including one of the deputy prime ministers.

Section 4. Corruption and Lack of Transparency in Government

The law provides criminal penalties for official corruption, but the government did not implement the law adequately, and some officials reportedly engaged in corrupt practices with impunity. The law subjects government employees at all levels to prosecution if they use their positions to engage in embezzlement or bribery, either directly or indirectly. Penalties can be up to 10 years' imprisonment.

Corruption: The Bahrain National Audit Office is responsible for combating government corruption. In November the government released segments of its report to the press, which published parts of it; however, the full report was not published or made available online as of year's end. The report noted the government's failure to stay within allocated budget amounts. On May 31, parliamentarians discussed items mentioned in the 2015 report, but they did not release the full report to the public.

Significant areas of government activity, including the security services and the Bahrain Defense Force, lacked transparency, and the privatization of public land continued to be a concern among opposition groups.

Financial Disclosure: The law does not require government officials to make financial disclosures.

Public Access to Information: Through its e-government portal, launched in 2007 but recently expanded, the government provided information about a variety of public stakeholders. For example, individuals were able to access information on travel bans, court cases, utility bills, student exam results, the government's budget, and other information. Individual ministries also maintained websites of varying qualities, which provided a wide range of information specific to that ministry.

Section 5. Governmental Attitude Regarding International and Nongovernmental Investigation of Alleged Violations of Human Rights

Government officials sometimes met with local human rights NGOs but generally were not responsive to the views of NGOs they believed were politicized and unfairly critical of the government.

Domestic human rights groups operated with some government restrictions. These groups included the Bahrain Human Rights Society, the primary independent and licensed human rights organization in the country; the Bahrain Center for Human Rights, which the government officially dissolved in 2004 but continued to operate and maintained an online presence; and the unlicensed Bahrain Youth Society for Human Rights. The unlicensed umbrella human rights organization Bahrain Human Rights Observatory also issued numerous reports and had strong ties to international human rights NGOs. The licensed Bahrain Human Rights Watch continued to issue numerous reports.

Some domestic human rights groups faced significant difficulties operating freely and interacting with international human rights organizations. The government sometimes harassed and deprived local NGO leaders of due process. Local NGO leaders and activists also reported government harassment including the imposition of travel bans (see section 2.c.), police surveillance, delayed processing of civil documents, and "inappropriate questioning" of their children during interviews for government scholarships.

Individuals affiliated with international human rights and labor organizations, or who were critical of the government, reported authorities indefinitely delayed or refused visa applications, or at times refused entry to the country for individuals who possessed a valid visa or qualified for the country's visa-free entry program.

In April authorities denied a Solidarity Center representative entry into the country although the individual possessed a valid visa. The purpose of the trip was to meet with a domestic labor organization.

Government Human Rights Bodies: In 2011 the government convened the BICI, chaired by Cherif Bassiouni, whose staff included international human rights experts, and tasked it with investigating allegations of human rights violations-- including reports of police brutality, arrests, disappearances, and torture, along with reports of violence by demonstrators against police--in early 2011. It presented recommendations for reform in late 2011, describing a "culture of impunity" in the security services and documenting excessive use of force, including torture and a range of other human rights violations by security forces during the unrest. On May 9, Bassiouni returned to Bahrain on an unannounced visit to meet with the king and the national commission and received an award. The BNA reported that Bahrain had fully implemented the recommendations of the BICI report and suggested Bassiouni concurred. On June 5, Bassiouni published a statement on his website recognizing Bahrain's accomplishments on BICI implementation, but he made clear his view that the country has not yet fulfilled all of the recommendations of the BICI report. Among outstanding recommendations, Bassiouni said that Bahrain should prioritize the release of prisoners convicted on the basis of their political beliefs and expression and emphasize accountability for those responsible for deaths resulting from torture.

In line with the 2011 BICI report recommendations, the king issued a royal decree in 2013 to re-establish the country's National Human Rights Organization, now called the NIHR, to receive complaints and investigate allegations of human rights violations. Throughout the year the NIHR conducted numerous human rights workshops, seminars, and training sessions, as well as prison visits, and referred numerous complaints to the PPO. It issued its latest annual report in December 2015 and contributed to PDRC, ombudsman, and SIU investigations. Also in December an amendment to the law strengthened the NIHR by giving it the right to conduct unannounced visits to police facilities and increasing its financial independence. Although many observers viewed the NIHR as effectively resourced and independent, other human rights groups doubted the government would implement most of its recommendations and doubted its impartiality.

During the year the government also maintained the Ombudsman's Office within the Ministry of Interior, the SIU within the PPO, and the PDRC in response to the BICI report's recommendations. These organizations worked with each other throughout the year.

Local and international observers and human rights organizations continued to view the BICI report as a standard against which to measure the country's progress on human rights reforms. They expressed concern the government did not make significant progress on other BICI recommendations, including dropping charges against individuals engaged in nonviolent political expression, criminally charging security officers accused of abuse or torture, integrating Shia into security forces, and creating an environment conducive to national reconciliation.

Section 6. Discrimination, Societal Abuses, and Trafficking in Persons

Women

<u>Rape and Domestic Violence</u>: Rape is illegal. The law does not address spousal rape. Penalties for rape include life imprisonment and execution in cases where the victim is a minor younger than 16 years old or in cases where the rape leads to the victim's death. From January through August, the PPO referred 73 cases of sexual harassment, which can include rape, to courts. The Migrant Workers Protection Society (MWPS) temporarily sheltered approximately 150 women, most of whom were domestic workers, including at least one woman who reported rape. The MWPS estimated hundreds of cases went unreported because domestic workers had difficulty leaving their places of work, or might not possess their passports or other identification needed to open a case.

No government policies or laws explicitly address domestic violence. Human rights organizations alleged spousal abuse of women was widespread. According to the BCHR, 30 percent of women had experienced some form of domestic abuse. Women rarely sought legal redress for violence due to fear of social reprisal or stigma. Authorities devoted little public attention to the problem. The government maintained the Dar al-Aman Shelter for women and children who were victims of domestic violence. The shelter had 16 apartments with accommodations for two women in each apartment. The shelter accommodated citizens and noncitizens and provided transportation for children to attend schools. Authorities stationed a policewoman at the shelter, which authorities did not identify on its exterior, to provide security. Victims of domestic violence had difficulty knowing who to contact or how to proceed when filing a complaint. Procedures required interviews of both the victim and the accused at the same police station; there were no provisions in place to prevent accused family members from having access to their victims.

<u>Other Harmful Traditional Practices</u>: "Honor" killings are punishable under the law, but the penal code provides a lenient sentence for the killing of a spouse caught in the act of adultery, whether male or female. There were no reports of honor killings during the year.

<u>Sexual Harassment</u>: The law prohibits sexual harassment, including insulting or committing an indecent act towards a woman in public, with penalties of prison and fines. The government reported that from January through August, there were 268 cases of reported sexual harassment, and the PPO transferred 73 to court. Of those cases 25 resulted in convictions; the remaining cases were pending at year's end. Although the government sometimes enforced the law, sexual harassment remained a widespread problem for women, especially foreigners employed as domestic workers and in other low-level service jobs.

<u>Reproductive Rights</u>: Couples and individuals have the right to decide the number, spacing, and timing of children; manage their reproductive health; and have access to the information and means to do so, free from discrimination, coercion, or violence. Health centers required women to obtain spousal consent to undergo sterilization; this consent requirement did not apply for provision of other family planning services.

<u>Discrimination</u>: Women faced discrimination under the law. A woman cannot transmit nationality to her spouse or children (see section 2.d., Stateless Persons). Women have the right to initiate divorce proceedings, but both Shia and Sunni religious courts may refuse the request, although the refusal rate was significantly higher in Shia courts than in Sunni courts, with Shia courts often refusing to grant the divorce due to differences in legal codes. In divorce cases the courts routinely granted mothers custody of daughters younger than age nine and sons younger than age seven. Custody usually reverted to the father once girls and boys reached the ages of nine and seven, respectively. Regardless of custody decisions, the father retains guardianship, or the right to make all legal decisions for the child, until a child reaches the age of 21. A noncitizen woman automatically loses custody of her children if she divorces their citizen father "without just cause."

The basis for family law is sharia as interpreted by Sunnis and Shia. Only Sunni family law is codified, while Shia maintain separate judicial bodies composed of religious jurisprudents charged with interpreting sharia. It was not always clear which courts have jurisdiction in Sunni-Shia marriages.

Women may own and inherit property and represent themselves in all public and legal matters. In the absence of a direct male heir, Shia women may inherit all of their husband's property, while Sunni women inherit only a portion, as governed by sharia, and the brothers or other male relatives of the deceased divide the balance. Better-educated families used wills and other legal tools to mitigate the discriminatory effects of these rules.

Labor laws prohibit discrimination against women, but discrimination against women was systemic, especially in the workplace (see section 7.d.). The law prohibits wage discrimination based on gender. Although women held positions of authority in the government and private sector, they did not have proportional representation. Cultural barriers and religious tradition sometimes hampered women's rights.

On April 5, parliament passed a royal decree lifting all reservations on the Convention on the Elimination of all Forms of Discrimination Against Women.

Children

Birth Registration: Individuals derive citizenship from one's father or by decree from the king. Women cannot transmit their nationality to their children, rendering stateless some children of citizen mothers but noncitizen fathers (see section 2.d., Stateless Persons). Authorities do not register births immediately. From birth to the age of three months, the mother's primary health-care provider holds registration for the children. Upon reaching three months, authorities register the birth with the Ministry of Health's Birth Registration Unit, which then issues the official birth certificate. The birth certificate does not include the child's religion. Children not registered before reaching their first birthday must obtain a registration by court order. The government does not provide public services to a child without a birth certificate.

The wife of imprisoned Wifaq secretary general Sheikh Ali Salman was unable to get a passport and other civil documents for their young child while her husband was in prison. She reported that various authorities told her Salman would have to come into each of their offices in person to sign the applications. The Ministry of Interior did not facilitate transportation of prisoners to government offices to address administrative or financial matters, nor did it make these types of services available in detention facilities.

Education: Schooling is compulsory for children until age 15 and provided free of charge to citizens and legal residents through grade 12. Authorities segregated government-run schools by gender, although the schools educated girls and boys with the same curricula and textbooks. Islamic studies based on Sunni doctrine are mandatory for all Muslim public school students and are optional for non-Muslim students; however, there is little provision for parents to request alternate religious instruction, including for the large population of Shia enrolled in public schools.

Child Abuse: NGOs reported an increase in child abuse cases in recent years, but they were unsure whether it reflected increases in abuse or greater willingness to report it. Sharia courts, not civil courts, address crimes involving child abuse, including violence against children. NGOs expressed concern over the lack of consistently written guidelines for prosecuting and punishing offenders and the leniency of penalties in child abuse cases. As of August the PPO reported 67 sexual harassment cases registered where the victim was a child. In August the

Ministry of Social Development reported it had helped 335 children since the beginning of the year, and its child abuse hotline had received 1,200 calls.

There were reports police approached children outside of schools and threatened or coerced them into becoming police informants.

Early and Forced Marriage: According to the law, the minimum age of marriage is 15 years old for girls and 18 years old for boys, but special circumstances allow marriages below these ages with approval from a sharia court. The government made concerted efforts to draw attention to the dangers of early marriage for girls and the adverse effect on children's health.

Sexual Exploitation of Children: The law prohibits exploitation of a child for various crimes, including prostitution. Penalties include imprisonment of no less than three months if the accused used exploitation and force to commit the crime and up to six years if the accused exploited more than one child, as well as penalties of at least 2,000 dinars ($5,400) for individuals and at least 10,000 dinars ($27,000) for organizations. Penalties vary depending on the specific law involved. The law also prohibits child pornography. There is no minimum age for consensual sex, as the law assumes there is no consensual sex outside of marriage.

International Child Abductions: The country is not a party to the 1980 Hague Convention on the Civil Aspects of International Child Abduction. See the Department of State's *Annual Report on International Parental Child Abduction* at travel.state.gov/content/childabduction/en/legal/compliance.html.

Anti-Semitism

According to community members, there were between 36 and 40 Jewish citizens (six families) in the country. Some anti-Jewish political commentary and editorial cartoons occasionally appeared in print and electronic media, usually linked to the Israeli-Palestinian conflict, without government response.

Trafficking in Persons

See the Department of State's *Trafficking in Persons Report* at www.state.gov/j/tip/rls/tiprpt/.

Persons with Disabilities

The law stipulates equal treatment for persons with disabilities with regard to employment, and violations of the law are punishable with fines. It was unclear whether the government enforced these laws. According to the government, it re-established in 2012 a committee originally formed in 2011 to care for persons with disabilities and included representatives from all relevant ministries, NGOs, and the private sector. The committee is responsible for monitoring violations against persons with disabilities; it was unclear whether the committee acted on any incidents during the year.

Authorities mandated a variety of governmental, quasi-governmental, and religious institutions to support and protect persons with disabilities. New public buildings in the central municipality must include facilities for persons with disabilities. The law, however, does not outline specific criteria for what authorities required for facilities to be accessible for persons with disabilities. The law does not mandate access to other nonresidential buildings for persons with disabilities. There was no information available regarding a law providing access for persons with disabilities to information and communication.

There was no information available on the responsibilities of government agencies to protect the rights of persons with disabilities or on actions taken by government agencies to improve respect for their rights. According to anecdotal evidence, however, such persons routinely lacked access to education and employment. The one government school for children with hearing disabilities did not operate past the 10th grade. Some public schools had specialized education programs for children with learning disabilities, physical disabilities, speech disabilities, and Down syndrome, but the government did not fund private programs for children who could not find appropriate programs in public schools.

Eligible voters can vote either in their regular precincts or in a general polling station. The local precincts, which are mostly in schools, sometimes offered problems to those with mobility disabilities; however, the general polling stations are in public spaces such as malls, which allow for assistance devices. One candidate with disabilities in the 2014 parliamentary election complained that access restrictions separated him from the other candidates at a function, as there was no ramp for him to access the stage as a wheelchair user. There were also complaints there were no provisions made for those who were restricted to their house or a hospital to vote, as there was no absentee ballot system.

The law requires the government to provide vocational training for persons with disabilities who wish to work. The law also requires employers of more than 100 persons to hire at least 2 percent of its employees from the government's list of workers with disabilities. The government did not monitor compliance. The government placed persons with disabilities in some public-sector jobs.

In 2013 the minister of social development and chairperson for the High Committee for Persons with Disabilities, Fatima Mohammed al-Balooshi, announced the launch of a National Strategy for the Rights of Persons with Disabilities in cooperation with the UN Development Program. At year's end the Ministry of Labor and Social Development continued to work with the UN agency on support activities connected to the strategy.

National/Racial/Ethnic Minorities

The law grants citizenship to Arab applicants who have resided in the country for 15 years and non-Arab applicants who have resided in the country for 25 years. There was a lack of transparency in the naturalization process, and there were numerous reports authorities did not apply the citizenship law uniformly. There were allegations the government allowed foreign Sunni employees of the security services who had lived in the country for fewer than 15 years to apply for citizenship. There were also reports authorities had not granted citizenship to Arab Shia who had resided in the country for more than 15 years and non-Arab foreign residents who had resided more than 25 years. There were reports of general discrimination, especially in employment practices, against Shia citizens of Persian ethnicity (Ajam).

Although the government asserted the labor code for the private sector applies to all workers, the International Labor Organization (ILO) and international NGOs noted foreign workers faced discrimination in the workplace (see section 7).

Acts of Violence, Discrimination, and Other Abuses Based on Sexual Orientation and Gender Identity

The law does not criminalize same-sex sexual activity between consenting persons who are at least 21 years of age. Society did not accept lesbian, gay, bisexual, transgender, and intersex (LGBTI) activities, such as same-sex relationships and same-sex sexual activity, and discrimination based on sexual orientation or gender identity occurred. There were no open manifestations of LGBTI activity in the country, such as gay pride parades. On rare occasions courts approved the issuance of new legal documents for those who have undergone gender reassignment surgeries. In September, Bahrain TV aired a program discussing the legal rights and procedures of transgender individuals who wish to transition.

In April, two female students were arrested and sentenced to one-month in jail for kissing in a car. In September police raided a private party in Sanad and arrested 54 men for engaging in "obscene acts." In November the court acquitted 26 and sentenced 26 to one-month and two to three-months in jail.

HIV and AIDS Social Stigma

The media reported few cases of HIV/AIDS. There were no known reports of societal violence or discrimination against persons based on HIV/AIDS status, but medical experts acknowledged publicly that discrimination existed. The government mandated screening of newly arrived migrant workers for infectious diseases, including HIV/AIDS. At times in the past, the government deported migrant workers found to be HIV/AIDS positive, but the status of deportations during the year was unclear.

Other Societal Violence and Discrimination

The Ministry of Social Development continued to implement its national social and economic reconciliation plan Wi'da Wa'da. The ministry funded 20 local NGOs to promote reconciliation and solidarity and organized periodic workshops related to national unity and communication between all parties. The ministry established a High Committee for Advising Youth and Resolving Criminal Cases for youth involved in violent activity. The committee sought to limit children's participation in violent protests. Its strategy included organizing family consultations, assuring that students attend school, and holding parents responsible for their children's behavior.

The government's 2013 BICI follow-up report noted the Ministry of Education continued to work with UNESCO experts on incorporating human rights principles in textbooks. The report also indicated the ministry had signed cooperation agreements with the International Bureau of Education in Geneva.

Section 7. Worker Rights

a. Freedom of Association and the Right to Collective Bargaining

The constitution and labor code recognize the right to form independent trade unions and the right to strike, with significant restrictions. The law does not provide for the right to collective bargaining.

The law prohibits trade unions in the public sector. Public-sector workers may join private-sector trade unions and professional associations, although these entities cannot bargain on their behalf. The law also prohibits members of the military services and domestic workers from joining unions. Foreign workers, who comprised approximately 60 percent of the workforce, may join unions if they work in a sector that allows unions, although the law reserves union leadership roles for citizens. The law prohibits unions from engaging in political activities and requires all trade unions to affiliate with one of the country's two legal federations, the General Federation of Bahrain Trade Unions (GFBTU) or the Bahrain Free Labor Union Federation (BFLUF).

The law specifies only a trade union can organize and declare legal strikes and imposes excessive requirements for legal strikes. The law prohibits strikes in 10 "vital" sectors--the scope of which exceeds international standards--including the oil, gas, education, telecommunications, transportation, and health sectors, as well as in pharmacies and bakeries. The law makes no distinction between "vital" and "nonvital" employees within these sectors. Workers must approve a strike with a simple majority by secret ballot and provide 15 days' notification to the employer before conducting a strike.

A 2012 law significantly amended the labor code as it pertains to trade unions and federations. The law allows multiple trade union federations but prohibits multisector labor federations and bars individuals convicted of violating criminal laws that lead to trade union or executive council dissolution from holding union leadership posts. The amendment gives the minister of labor, rather than the unions, the right to select the federation to represent workers in national-level bargaining and international forums. In 2014 authorities amended the private-sector labor law, replacing "GFBTU" wherever it appeared in the legislation with the phrase "the appropriate federation designated by the minister of labor." The law does not prohibit antiunion discrimination, nor does it require reinstatement of workers fired for union activity.

The government generally respected freedom of association for workers. Relations between the main federations and the Ministry of Labor were publicly contentious at times. The government sometimes interfered in GFBTU activities. The GFBTU alleged that the government intended the legal amendments allowing the minister of labor to select a representative union to undermine its position as the country's representative labor federation.

Following a revision to the law, which provides for multiple trade union federations, in 2012 authorities established a second federation, BFLUF. The ministry had consistently designated the GFBTU as the country's representative, but in 2015 it designated the BFLUF to represent the country before the Arab Labor Organization. Some workers and union affiliates complained union pluralism had resulted in company management interfering in union dues collection and workers' chosen union affiliation and in management choosing to negotiate with the union they found most favorable--to the detriment of existing collective bargaining agreements and the legitimate voice of workers.

During the year the government made efforts to provide for the reinstatement of workers dismissed or suspended during the 2011 State of National Safety. It continued working with the tripartite committee, formed in 2011 and consisting of a representative from the Ministry of Labor, the Bahrain Chamber of Commerce and Industry, and GFBTU, to address dismissals and reinstatements as part of the government's response to recommendations set forth in the 2011 BICI. In 2014, after signing a second tripartite agreement, the ILO dismissed the complaint filed in 2011. This agreement identified 165 cases to be resolved, and all parties reported positive progress on those reinstatements. Some reinstated workers, however, alleged some companies insisted they sign loyalty pledges and agreements to not strike, despite such requirements being illegal. Workers reported many cases of discrimination in hiring and promotion, including in the public sector. Some civil service employees, including in the Ministry of Education, reported authorities questioned them about their outside activities.

On July 17, hundreds of foreign construction workers went on strike over unpaid salaries. The Ministry of Labor and Social Development intervened and announced on July 24 that the situation had been resolved with the company providing its employees the money they were owed.

b. Prohibition of Forced or Compulsory Labor

The law prohibits all forms of forced or compulsory labor except in national emergencies, and the government did not always enforce the law effectively. There were reports of forced labor in the construction and service sectors. The labor law covers foreign workers, except domestic workers, but enforcement was lax, and cases of debt bondage were common. There were also reports forced labor practices occurred among domestic workers and others working in the informal sector; labor laws did not protect most of these workers. In 2012 the government amended the labor law to provide domestic workers the right to see their terms of employment.

In many cases employers withheld passports, restricted movement, substituted contracts, or did not pay wages; some employers also threatened workers and subjected them to physical and sexual abuse. The Ministry of Labor reported complaints from domestic workers, mostly of unpaid wages. In 2013 the Ministry of Social Development took steps to fulfill its legal obligation under the trafficking in persons law to identify and protect foreign victims of trafficking, including by creating comprehensive guidelines and training government officials on the framework to protect trafficking victims.

Estimates of the proportion of migrant workers in the country under illegal "free visa" arrangements--a practice that can contribute to debt bondage--ranged from 10 to 25 percent. In numerous cases employers withheld salaries from foreign workers for months or years and refused to grant them permission to leave the country. Fear of deportation or employer retaliation prevented many foreign workers from complaining to authorities.

The Labor Market Regulatory Authority (LMRA) took steps to reduce the vulnerability of foreign workers. It instituted procedures that allowed workers to change the employer associated with their visa either without permission from their old employer or without being in possession of their passport. LMRA threatened employers who withheld passports with criminal and administrative violations, and prohibited at-fault employers from hiring new workers.

On January 3, the LMRA announced that the amnesty from July through December 2015, aimed at allowing workers without work permits to legalize their presence in Bahrain or return home without being "blacklisted," had succeeded in helping more than 40,000 workers. Of those who submitted documents, 30,000 opted to stay in Bahrain and found new employers to sponsor them, while 10,000 returned to their home countries.

Also see the Department of State's *Trafficking in Persons Report* at www.state.gov/j/tip/rls/tiprpt/.

c. Prohibition of Child Labor and Minimum Age for Employment

The minimum age for employment is 15 years, and the minimum age for hazardous work is 18. Children under 18 may not work in industries the Ministry of Health deemed hazardous or unhealthy, including construction, mining, and oil refining. Minors under the age of 18 may work no more than six hours a day--no more than four days consecutively--and may be present on the employment premises no more than seven hours a day. The Ministry of Labor made rare exceptions on a case-by-case basis for juveniles age 14 or 15, who had an urgent need to assist in providing financial support for their families. Child labor regulations do not apply to family-operated businesses in which the only other employees are family members.

A 2012 labor law requires that before the Labor Ministry makes a final decision on allowing a minor to work, the prospective employer must present documentation from the minor's guardian giving the minor permission to work, proof the minor underwent a physical fitness examination to confirm suitability, and assurance from the employer the minor would not work in an environment the ministry deemed hazardous. Generally, the government effectively enforced the law.

There were some non-Bahraini children employed as domestic servants. Observers believed some Bahraini children worked in family-run businesses, but the practice did not appear widespread.

Also see the Department of Labor's *Findings on the Worst Forms of Child Labor* at www.dol.gov/ilab/reports/child-labor/findings/.

d. Discrimination with Respect for Employment and Occupation

The constitution provides for equality between men and women in political, social, cultural, and economic spheres without breaching the provisions of Islamic canon law. There are no specific protections regarding race, disability, language, sexual orientation and/or gender identity, HIV-positive status or having other communicable diseases, or social status. The government lacked any specific implementing regulations or processes to identify proactively cases of discrimination or to address and seek remedy for any cases of which they might become aware.

The government took steps to promote women's participation in the workforce, although women continued to face discrimination there, especially in fields traditionally dominated by men, including leadership positions. Women reported having to work harder than men to be recognized at work; they often faced hiring discrimination because of a perception they would become pregnant or their family lives would interfere with their work.

The Ministry of Social Development continued to fund the Disabled Services Center, which helped train and find work for Bahrainis with disabilities. It remained rare, however, for persons with disabilities to find employment in positions of responsibility. Many workplaces remained difficult to access for those needing assistance due to a lack of ramps, narrow doorways, and unpaved parking lots.

Many of the workers in the country were foreign workers. There are no provisions to provide for equality in the hiring process. It was common for employers to advertise positions for specific nationalities or languages without justifying why only persons from that specific nationality or language group would be acceptable. Even for blue-collar jobs, such as those in fast-food restaurants, it was common for employers to hire lower-level employees from one nationality and managerial staff from a second nationality.

Government institutions sometimes based their hiring decisions on a person's nationality, often without regard to qualifications. Some Bahraini teachers complained authorities ignored them for public school teaching jobs because authorities hired foreign teachers instead. Well-qualified Bahrainis reported being paid less than certain foreign workers because those workers were of a preferred nationality.

Lack of transparency in hiring processes, especially for government positions, led to many complaints of discrimination based on sect or ethnicity. Human rights organizations reported managers sometimes did not hire qualified applicants because of the neighborhoods where they lived or their family names.

Shia reported unemployment in their communities was much higher than government estimates. Several international firms reported pressure not to promote Shia to positions of responsibility within their companies. Shia perceived that employers subjected them to different standards and that employers were more likely to fire them. Sunni citizens often received preference for employment in sensitive government positions, notably in the managerial ranks of the civil service and the military. Shia asserted they were unable to obtain government positions, especially in the security services, because of their religious affiliation. There were reports during the year that Shia were also discriminated against when they applied for medical positions at institutions associated with the military such as the Bahrain Defense Force and King Hamad hospitals.

e. Acceptable Conditions of Work

There is no national private-sector minimum wage. A standardized government pay scale covers public-sector workers, with a set minimum of 300 dinars ($810) per month. Citizens who earned less received a government stipend to offset the difference. There is no minimum wage for foreign workers in the public sector, although the government issued "guidelines" advising employers in the public and private sectors to pay a minimum of 150 dinars per month ($405). There was no official poverty level.

Subject to the provisions of the private-sector law, employers may not employ a worker for more than 48 hours per week. Employers may not employ Muslim workers during the month of Ramadan for more than six hours per day or 36 hours per week. The standard workday is eight hours, with a maximum of 10 hours allowed. Overtime rates are time-and-a-quarter during the day and time-and-a-half during the evening. It is mandatory for workers to receive 24 consecutive hours off per week, and the day set for weekly rest is Friday. If employers require a worker to work on a mandatory rest day, employers will pay the worker at time-and-a-half. A worker may not work on mandatory rest days for two consecutive weeks without personal written consent.

The Ministry of Labor sets occupational safety and health standards. The labor law and relevant protections apply to citizens and noncitizens alike, with the exception of domestic workers. The revised labor law improved the legal situation for many workers as it pertains to access to contracts and additional holidays, although it excludes domestic workers from the majority of protections.

The Labor Ministry is responsible for enforcing the labor law and mandating acceptable conditions of work. During the year the government employed 23 labor inspectors and eight safety inspectors. The ministry enforced occupational safety and health standards; it also used a team of eight engineers from multiple specialties primarily to investigate risks and standards at construction sites, which were the vast majority of worksites.

Several circumstances prompt inspections: a complaint made to the ministry, notification of a new worksite made to the ministry, a media article about a new worksite, or discovery of a new worksite by an inspector in an assigned geographic area.

Inspectors have the authority to levy fines and close worksites if employers do not improve conditions by specified deadlines. Penalties for violators range from 500 dinars ($1,350) to 1,000 dinars ($2,700) per violation or per worker affected, or both, as determined by a judge. A judge may also sentence violators to a minimum of three months in prison. For repeat violators the court may double the penalties. The ministry reported an unspecified number of violators were serving sentences related to labor condition violations during the year.

Despite the improvements, NGOs feared resources for enforcement of the laws remained inadequate for the number of worksites and workers, that many worksites would not be inspected, and that the regulations would not necessarily deter violations.

A ministerial decree prohibits outdoor work between noon and 4 p.m. during July and August because of heat conditions. Authorities enforced the ban among large firms but, according to local sources, violations were common among smaller businesses. After inspecting 10,053 work sites, the Ministry of Labor reported 106 violations with 235 workers as victims. Employers who violated the ban are subject to up to three-months in jail, and a fine of 1,000 dinars ($2,700) fine; however, no information was made public about which employers violated the law, or what fine they were accessed, if any.

The government and courts generally worked to rectify abuses brought to their attention. Workers could lodge complaints with the Ministry of Labor. The ministry reported it received 2,684 complaints in 2015, the last year information was available. Labor officials stated they resolved most cases through mediation. By law authorities who cannot settle complaints through arbitration must refer them to the court within 15 days. The vast majority of cases involving abused domestic workers did not reach the ministry or the public prosecutor.

In February the Ministry of Labor reported it had taken legal action against 112 labor accommodations since 2012 and that employers corrected 436 irregularities after inspections and warnings. In April 2015 the Ministry of Labor reported there were more than 3,000 registered labor camps housing more than 150,000 workers in the country. In 2015 the ministry inspected 1,300 accommodations and recorded 70 violations, but it did not make public its enforcement actions. Many workers lived in unregistered accommodations that ranged in quality from makeshift accommodations in parking garages, to apartments rented by employers from private owners, to family houses modified to accommodate many persons. Inspectors do not have the right to enter houses or apartment buildings not registered as work camps to inspect conditions. The Labor Ministry advised the Ministry of Works, Municipalities Affairs, and Urban Planning and the Ministry of Housing when it received complaints of poor conditions in such housing. The Migrant Workers Protection Society reported it visited unregistered camps and accommodations, including ones that were potentially dangerous, such as places with 35 persons sharing three rooms.

The government continued to conduct workers' rights awareness campaigns. It published pamphlets on foreign resident workers' rights in several languages, provided manuals on these rights to local diplomatic missions, and operated a telephone hotline for victims.

Violations of wage, overtime, and occupational safety and health standards were common in sectors employing foreign workers, such as construction, automotive repair, and domestic service. Unskilled foreign workers, mostly from South and Southeast Asia, constituted approximately 60 percent of the total workforce (76 percent of the private-sector workforce). These workers were also vulnerable to dangerous or exploitive working conditions. According to NGOs, workplace safety inspection and compliance were substandard.

Local sources reported that lack of awareness of terms of employment remained a problem. Some foreign workers arrived in the country at the invitation of an employer who sponsored their visas but then switched jobs. Some of these workers continued to pay a portion of their salaries to their former employer who continued to be legally responsible for their visas.

The labor law does not fully protect domestic workers, and this group was particularly vulnerable to exploitation. In 2012 the government amended the labor law to expand the rights of domestic employees, not covered under the previous law. The labor law requires domestic employees have an agreement with their employer with "clear contractual terms" and provides penalties for violators. The amendments, however, do not accord domestic employees many of the rights the law provides to other private-sector workers, including limits on daily and weekly working hours, and rest days.

There were credible reports employers forced many of the country's 70,000 domestic workers, most of them women, to work from 12- to 16-hour days and surrender their identity documents to employers. Employers permitted very little time off; left them malnourished; and subjected them to verbal and physical abuse, including sexual molestation and rape. Reports of employers and recruitment agents beating or sexually abusing foreign women working in domestic positions were common. The press, embassies, and police received numerous reports of abuse.

The vast majority of cases involving abused domestic workers did not reach the Ministry of Labor or PPO for a variety of reasons. Most victims were too intimidated to sue their employers, although they had the right to do so. Some NGOs and activists reported that workers involved in a dispute with their employer were given the option to either leave the country or face jail time if the employer filed a counter-suit against them; in many cases the worker left the country, and the potentially abusive employer was able to bring in additional domestic workers with no repercussions. NGOs also reported the court system made it difficult for workers, who frequently did not have permanent home addresses in the country, to receive notices about their cases once they filed them. Additionally, if employees needing visa sponsorship filed a case against their employers, they were unable to request a transfer of their sponsorship to a new employer. If employees stayed in the country, they could work for other employers unofficially. Once they departed the country, however, they could not get a work visa with a new sponsor until authorities resolved the case with the previous employer.

During the year the MWPS shelter provided more than 150 female domestic workers with temporary housing and assistance with their cases. The majority of women in these cases sought assistance with unpaid wages and complaints of physical abuse. The MWPS continued to support victims who took their cases to court, but by law victims can receive only outstanding unpaid wages; no criminal damages are possible unless the victim has alleged a crime found in the criminal penal code has occurred, such as physical abuse or rape. While NGOs confirmed some cases were successful, compensation was meager. The government-run Dar al-Aman shelter moved to a new facility co-located with a branch of the LMRA and an office that runs a multilingual 24-hour help line for domestic workers who are abused.

The Ministry of Labor did not make public the number of deaths or injuries in workplace accidents. There were social media and press reports throughout the year, however, including the March 4 death of a cleaner on board a ship, and March 31 and November 9 reports on the deaths of two construction workers. Worker deaths generally were due to a combination of inadequate enforcement of standards, violations of standards, inadequate safety procedures, worker ignorance of those procedures, and inadequate safety standards for equipment. According to NGO sources, most accidents were in the construction sector, which employed more Bangladeshis and Pakistanis than other nationalities.

The MWPS noted suicide attempts were common among Indian workers but claimed the media underreported them.

Conditions in the many unregistered or illegal worker camps were often poor. Safety of accommodations and quality of life for workers were problems that continued to be a major concern at source-country embassies.

While some workers can remove themselves from situations that endanger health or safety without jeopardizing their employment, the level of freedom workers enjoyed directly related to the type of work they do. Foreign laborers and domestic workers have the most difficulty removing themselves from dangerous situations and have the fewest protections from firing. Both sets of workers relied on employers not just for housing but also for food, clothing, and transportation. They were also the least equipped to file a complaint due to language barriers, level of education, and inability to produce a government-issued identification card, which many employers retain.